Antonio Montes Orozco

Agile Coaching for Scrum Masters

Learn the main concepts of Coaching that Scrum Masters need to know

Table of Contents

Introduction 3
Definitions and Previous Principles 5
Trust 15
Listening 18
The Ladder of Inference 25
Nonviolent Communication 36
Feedback 47
Observer OSAR Model 52
Methodologies to Generate Action Plans 57
Questions 64
The Change of Beliefs 67
Examples of Coaching Sessions 78
How to "Be" a Coach 89
Conclusion 101
Special Thanks 102
About the Author 103
Credits 104

Antonio Montes Orozco

Introduction

In the Agile Scrum framework, the role of Scrum Master is the team leader, who must have a deep understanding of Scrum to be able to teach it to the team, acting as a mentor for it. In addition, they must have a series of conversational skills typical of Coaching, in order to motivate the team and lead it to high performance. Therefore, the Scrum Master is both a mentor (teacher) and a coach (motivator).

In this book I explain the conversational skills that every Scrum Master needs to have to become a great motivator for change in the team they lead.

I hope that, with these new tools, you will lead your team to high performance.

To get the most out of this book, you need to know the Agile philosophy and, specifically, the Scrum framework. If not, I recommend reading my first book, *Scrum for Non-Techies*.

Antonio Montes Orozco

Dedicated to:

Alejandro Polo and Fernando Vargas, for the constant support they've given to me

Antonio Montes Orozco

Definitions and Previous Principles

WITHOUT INVOLVEMENT THERE IS NO COMMITMENT

This is the key principle around which all 'Agilism' (which is how I define the Agile movement) and the entire philosophy of Coaching revolves. This key principle teaches us that, for the individual to commit to an action, they must participate in the decision that leads to undertaking that action. Its creator is Stephen Covey, author of the famous book *The 7 Habits of Highly Effective People*.

The immediate consequence of this principle is that hierarchical orders generate low-quality actions, since the subordinates who undertake them are not committed. If we want high-quality actions undertaken from the commitment, it is necessary to let the subordinate participate in the decision-making process.

The second consequence of this principle is that change cannot be born from a piece of advice given to us, but from our own reflection. This is the key to Coaching. The coach doesn't intend to give advice, but to make us reflect so that we realize what we need. Only through full involvement in the decision to undertake an action will we commit to carry it out. In short: the motivation for our action must lie in our own reflection.

Antonio Montes Orozco

DEFINITION OF COACH AND COACHING

After introducing Stephen Covey's principle and clarifying what motivates us to act, we can now define what it is that is so fashionable, the thing that we call Coaching.

One of the institutions that regulates the Coach profession is the ICF (International Coach Federation). This institution defines **Coaching** as "partnering with clients in a thought-provoking and creative process that inspires them to maximize their personal and professional potential". Therefore, a coach is not a counselor, but an inspirer and motivator who accompanies us in our reflections to reach our full potential.

From this definition we can begin to realize what qualities are necessary to motivate someone without counseling. The first thing is **knowing how to listen**. This is difficult because, dear reader, in our societies we are not taught to listen. When someone speaks to us, we are constantly applying our filters and beliefs, issuing judgments and opinions, or we are looking forward to intervening to show off our wisdom, so we are wanting our interlocutor to finish so that we can speak. Many discussions with our partner or with coworkers have their origin in this ignorance that we don't know how to listen properly.

We already know that the coach is an expert listener, but how are they going to make us reflect? How do they make us realize our possibilities? All this is achieved through **questions**. The purpose of a "Powerful Question" is to put our entire brain in the right disposition to make a choice and commit to an action.

Listening and answering the questions that the coach asks us will lead us to realize our needs and to look for a plan of action. Therefore, the third skill that the coach must have is to know **methodologies to generate action plans** and carry them out. There we will see the **GROW** methodology, and another simpler one that I have named **FCA**.

To open our hearts to the questions that the coach asks us, we must have great trust. This brings us to the last, great skill that the coach must possess, and that is **to be trustworthy**.

In short, the coach is a person in whom we fully trust, and who offers themself to us body and soul to listen to us, understands us, empathizes with us and, through 'Powerful Questions', help us become aware of ourselves in order to commit ourselves to concrete improvement actions. To help us undertake these improvement actions, the coach is an expert in methodologies to generate action plans and carry them out.

Now that we are clear about what a coach is, we can already distinguish what qualities they will have and which they won't. A coach will be a facilitator, a leader, a companion, a belief detector, and a person who, above all, generates **trust**. On the other hand, a coach is not a psychologist, nor a consultant, nor a confessor, nor the protagonist of the conversation.

Antonio Montes Orozco

THE LANGUAGE

Coaching includes the following three postulates about language:

- Humans are linguistic beings. That is, they express their ideas through words.

- The **fallacy** of **descriptive language**. Language not only describes but "creates reality". This leads us to be extremely careful with it, since we can eliminate the possibility of improvement by using victimizing language. In this way, **language ceases to be innocent**. From now on you will have to monitor how the team uses language to avoid falling into victimization and to be able to follow a path of "Continuous Improvement". Later on I will explain what victimizing language is and how language influences our way of thinking.

- Human beings **create themselves through language**. For example, if I label myself as "unable to change," I'll never be able to change, and I'll take a reactive victim stance toward life. However, if I label myself as "capable of improvement," I'll continually improve and take a proactive and responsible stance toward life.

Language has four acts:

- **Affirmations**. The affirmation embodies a piece of data or fact of the reality that surrounds us. For example: "Our team's sprints last four weeks."

- **Declarations**. The declaration sets out the vision for the future, thus facilitating Continuous Improvement aimed at achieving this vision. For example, if the vision is to become a high-performing team that completes the project on time, rest assured that Continuous Improvement will help achieve this. The most famous declaration ever made was when, in 1962, in the midst of the Cold War with the USSR, then-President John F. Kennedy declared his intention that the US would **reach the moon** before the end of the decade. And they more than succeeded.

- **Petitions**. The petitions reflect our needs or our team's. You have to know how to detect them and seek help through a petition. Later we will see how to make requests through Nonviolent Communication.

- **Offers**. When a need is detected in our interlocutor, an offer can be posed that covers the aforementioned need. Requests and offers connect need and commitment.

DEFINITION OF 'DISTINCTION'

In the end, if we are talking about knowing how to listen and knowing how to ask, we find that a coach is an expert in holding conversations. And, in conversations, language is the key part. Hence, it is necessary to introduce the definition of the word **"distinction"** for Coaching. The distinctions of the same reality are the different words that can define it, according to the nuances that we want to emphasize. For example, to describe the ways in which water is present in nature, we have the distinctions river, stream, torrent, tributary, sea, ocean, lake, puddle, rain, hurricane, etc. It is not the same to refer to a river, which already has a connotation of high flow, as a stream, which has a connotation of low flow. Therefore, it is very interesting to know the "distinctions" of language, as they expand our mental model.

I will introduce different distinctions as I progress in my exposition so that you enrich your vocabulary. For example, I propose to you the first distinction for Agile.

DISTINCTION: AGILIST AND AGILISM

Agilism is how I call the philosophy contained in the Agile movement.

An **Agilist** is someone who practices Agile; that is, someone who practices Agilism.

I will use both words throughout this book. And, while we are at it, I present another distinction.

DISTINCTION: COACH AND COACHEE

Coach is the motivator, while **coachee** is the one who is helped and motivated by the coach.

MENTAL MODELS

Mental models are the internal representations of reality that we form throughout life, and that determines how we interpret the reality that surrounds us. In the same way, they influence the decisions we make and can make us feel, in totally different ways, similar situations. Therefore, mental models are like the operating system that our brain works with; they are formed by the beliefs we have, and they are the lenses through which we see the world.

We can only influence what we can observe, and mental models filter reality for us. Therefore, these models will condition our way of acting. Let's not forget that this is always done through Language.

Mental models are formed from the following factors:

- **The genetic**. The brain of each individual is unique and particular, as well as their way of processing information.

- **Personal experiences**. Experiences lived condition our way of thinking, acting, and feeling. For example, if we were bitten as children by a dog, we'll tend to think that these animals are dangerous, and we'll distrust each time we see one.

- **Culture**. Our social and cultural environment conditions us the way we interpret the data and the way in which we draw conclusions. For example, there are very aggressive family environments that invite us to be defensive and hope for the worst, while there are other family environments where manners are very kind and they tend to always hope for the best.

- **Communication channels**. Language and the way of using it influences mental models. For example, there are languages with prefixes and suffixes that add many nuances to adjectives, while other languages are more sparing. The more distinctions we know about the same concept, the richer our mental model will be and the more we can adjust to the objective data.

LACK OF TIME AS AN ENEMY OF THE COACH

The main enemy of the coach is lack of time. This lack of time prevents full dedication to listen and to inquire with Powerful Questions, making the coach regress to their old habits of judging or not listening.

If you cannot have that full dedication, it is preferable to postpone the conversation to a time when there are no interruptions. In this way, you will become predictable and you will be seen as someone trustworthy who, when listening, does so in a dedicated and full way.

I make this brief reference to the lack of time, because you will see that being a coach implies a Temperance out of the ordinary, which can be ruined by the rushing and lack of time. I'm very interested that you are aware that the conversations you handle have to be of quality, protecting them as much as possible, in order to listen properly and help.

SUMMARY

- **Without involvement there is no commitment**. Therefore, the coach seeks the participation and internal reflection of the coachee.

- The **coach** is a person in whom we fully trust, and who offers themself to us, body and soul, to listen to us, understand us, empathize with us and, through Powerful Questions, help us to become aware of ourselves to commit ourselves to concrete, improvement actions. To help us undertake these improvement actions, the coach is an expert in methodologies to generate action plans (GROW, FCA) and carry them out.

- We've talked about **Language**, seeing the human being as a linguistic being, who creates themself through Language. Language not only describes, but "creates reality". Therefore you have to be very careful with it.

- A **distinction** is the set of words that define the same reality, according to its nuances. For example, river, torrent, tributary and stream, applied to a stream of water. The distinctions enrich our language, which is the key element used in the conversations between the coach and the team.

- I have presented you with the first "distinction" in relation to Agile: **Agilist**, to refer to an Agile practitioner, and **Agilism**, to refer to the philosophy encompassed in the Agile Movement.

- I have presented a second "distinction" in relation to the roles of Coaching: **coach** is the one who helps and motivates, and **coachee** is the one who receives motivation and help from the coach.

- Mental models are the set of our beliefs, and they condition our way of seeing reality. Our genetics, personal experiences, our culture, and the communication channels we use (language) are involved in its formation.

- Whenever you have a conversation, protect the environment from interruptions. It is preferable to postpone the conversation until you are one hundred percent available.

- As a bibliography for this chapter, I recommend *The 7 Habits of Highly Effective People* by Stephen Covey.

Trust

THE PILLARS OF TRUST

We've seen that a coach is someone who, above all, generates trust. Therefore, a coach must try to create a context of **psychological safety**. The pillars of this context are the following:

- **Sincerity and transparency**. Trust is a treasure that is very difficult to obtain and very easy to lose. A coach has to be very sincere and transparent in order to gain the trust of the team. Sincerity implies never being untruthful. Transparency implies showing vulnerabilities and moods, so that there're no mistakes nor misunderstandings. Sincerity and transparency make the coach predictable, and that gives the team security. As a consequence, we deduce that the coach is someone with **high ethics and morality**.

- **Technical competence**. Three essential skills are presupposed to the coach: knowing how to listen, knowing how to ask, and knowing methodologies for generating and achieving action plans. A team that trusts in the abilities of its coach feels safe.

- **Connection with people**. The coach is empathetic and knows how to connect with the moods and needs of the team. This connection gives a lot of security to the team, as it feels understood.

- **Impeccability of commitments**. Keeping promises is an art in team performance. Therefore, the coach must have the competence to know how to make promises and to keep them. In addition, they will also have to take charge and take responsibility in case of non-compliance. A coach who always keeps their promises becomes very trustworthy to the team.

CONSEQUENCES OF LOSING TRUST

Trust within the team is a sacred asset that must be taken care of as much as possible because, if team members feel insecure (**absence of trust**), they will have **fear of conflict** and will stop participating in decisions, as they will have fear of reactions and consequences. If they stop participating they will stop committing (**lack of commitment**) to achieving goals (remember Stephen Covey's principle). If they stop committing to the achievement of objectives, they will stop taking responsibility for their colleagues (**avoidance of accountability**), ignoring the violation of established agreements, such as performing unit tests or doing work with the required quality. If they feel insecure, stop participating and do not take responsibility for their colleagues, in the end they will neglect the project (**inattention to results**) and will consider leaving the team.

These are the five dysfunctions that Patrick Lencioni, a famous American writer of business management books, described in his book *The Five Dysfunctions of a Team*. Note that everything starts with the absence of trust, ending in the destruction of the team and the failure of the project.

SUMMARY

— We've seen the pillars of the team's trust in its coach, presenting them as someone who, above all, generates trust. The bases for creating a context of psychological safety are:

- **Sincerity and transparency**. The coach never bends the truth and has no qualms about showing vulnerable.

- **Technical competence**. The coach knows how to listen, knows how to ask, and knows methodologies for the generation and achievement of action plans.

- **Connection with people**. The coach connects and empathizes with the team, detecting its needs.

- **Impeccability of commitments**. The coach always keeps their promises, and takes responsibility in case of breaking them.

— Finally, we've seen the direct consequences of losing trust, and I've presented the five dysfunctions of the teams as enunciated by Patrick Lencioni: **absence of trust, fear of conflict, lack of commitment, avoidance of accountability**, and **inattention to results**.

— As a reading, I recommend *The Five Dysfunctions of a Team* by Patrick Lencioni.

Listening

If we consider an Organization as a 'network of conversations' where offers and requests are made, we realize how important listening is. In listening we must not forget the part of interpretation. We must banish the idea that we all listen in the same way, because we are always filtering based on our beliefs and judgments, so we interpret in very different ways. There is always an "interpretive gap" that must be managed.

According to the effectiveness of listening, we can classify it into the following levels, from least to most effective:

LISTENING LEVELS

- **Ignoring**. It is directly not listening. This, apart from being of little use and leading our interlocutor to distrust, is rude. If we cannot listen to someone, it is much better to be predictable and, assertively and politely, communicate that at that moment we cannot listen. Let's remember that trust is a treasure that is difficult to obtain and very easy to lose.

- **Pretending**. We pretend to be listening, but we are really preoccupied on another matter. Pretending is an unethical way of acting and it makes people lose trust in us, that great treasure that is so hard to get. In this case, I advise we make ourselves predictable so as not to pretend, and thus gain the trust of our interlocutor: "Would you mind if we speak later? Now I'm busy, and later on I'll be able to give you all the attention you deserve." And now comes the question where we leave space for participation and commitment: "When is it good for you to talk?" Or this other one: "Would you like us to talk in half an hour?"

- **Previous**. Before our interlocutor finishes the sentence, we are applying prejudices and beliefs. These filters prevent us from listening to the objective data and facts that they are telling us. In addition, the previous listening is irritating for the interlocutor. This practice is an inexhaustible source of problems, both in our personal lives and in our professional ones.

- **Selective**. We focus only on what interests us. That can lead us to lose information that can be key. The important thing is not what interests us, but what the interlocutor is talking about. Humility is our great ally, and our Ego is our great ballast.

- **Active**. We try to understand everything that is said, and if we do not understand something, we ask for clarification. We also paraphrase to make sure that we have understood what the interlocutor has wanted to tell us. An example of a paraphrase would be the following: "I have understood you that the delivery date is brought forward by ten days and that the export module no longer has to be done. Is that so? Have I understood you correctly?" Although we have understood everything, in active listening we forget what the mood of our interlocutor means for what they are telling us. For this reason, it is necessary to take another leap in the level of listening.

- **Empathetic.** Not only do we actively listen and understand everything, but we also try to understand how the interlocutor feels and what the events they are talking about produce in them on an emotional level. This level of listening is one of the most perfect, but we still have a great presence of the self, which can lead us to filter and judge as soon as we are careless.

- **Egoless**. We give ourselves body and soul to listen to our interlocutor, forgetting about ourselves, avoiding selecting data and applying filters, focusing on understanding everything and empathizing with our interlocutor, and remembering ourselves just to verify that we continue listening with all our attention. It is the most generous and perfect listening that exists: it is almost an act of love and requires belief in the human being. Coaching, dear reader, is a source of ethical values that makes us better people, and we can learn a lot from it.

I have a joke with my colleagues, and it is that Coaching is almost like a Religion, since it provides us with a bomb-proof ethic and dedication to others, apart from encouraging us to be humble and put our Ego aside. The reward is the well-being caused by being able to help others, giving a lot of meaning to our work.

Antonio Montes Orozco

DISTINCTION: EMPATHY and SYMPATHY

It is important to be clear about the difference between empathic listening and sympathetic listening.

In **empathic listening** we connect with the interlocutor, to feel and vibrate in unison, maintaining objectivity. With empathic listening:

- We tend to connection. We vibrate with our interlocutor and we resonate together.

- We listen to understand. If we do not understand something, we ask to understand everything.

- We focus on emotion. We inquire what emotion our interlocutor feels regarding what they are talking about.

- It requires learning. We have to train ourselves to learn to listen empathically.

- The answer is non-verbal (we connect and vibrate with our interlocutor), so we use more body language.

- We do not judge. We limit ourselves to understanding the facts as well as the emotions they produce.

- It is not mutual (because it's only we who try to empathize).

- The conversation is kept on an emotional level, focusing on our interlocutor and their feelings.

In **sympathetic listening** we like the interlocutor, and therefore everything they say we will agree with, thus losing objectivity. It is a listening in which we will not be able to help anything. With sympathetic listening:

- We tend to disconnection, because we are going to agree with everything they tell us, so we do not mirror the emotion of our interlocutor.

- We listen to respond; above all to agree and emphasize our conformity.

- We seek approval; that is, that out of sympathy they agree with what we say.

- It is spontaneous, so it doesn't require training. This is the level of listening that we've learned since childhood.

- The answer is verbal. As there is no connection, we do not mirror the emotions of our interlocutor with our body, so the whole conversation focuses on Language.

- We judge. If our interlocutor is upset by someone's attitude, we can come to judge that someone.

- The sympathy is mutual, so in the end neither of us listens objectively.

- The conversation is kept on an intellectual rather than an emotional plane.

- It focuses on the words and the solution, ignoring the emotions.

Although we like our interlocutor, we can train ourselves to ignore our feelings, in order to be objective and focus empathically on what they feel without agreeing automatically. What's more, since we like them, we can help more if we do empathic listening, as we'll maintain objectivity.

It is important that the concept of empathy is clear. So I'm going to show you some examples of what empathy is not. **Empathy is not**:

- Advising: "I think you should…"

- Competing: "That's nothing, it happened to me that…"

- Educating: "This can be very positive for you."

- Comforting: "You did what you could."

- Minimizing: "It's not so bad…"

- Pitying: "Poor…!"

- Telling a similar story: "This reminds me that…"

- Explaining: "I would have come, but…"

- Correcting: "No, that did not happen like that…"

SUMMARY

— We've seen the Organization as a 'network of conversations' where offers and requests are made, hence the importance of knowing how to listen.

— Then we've seen the listening levels:

- **Ignoring**. We directly don't listen.

- **Pretending**. We pretend to be listening, but we are really paying attention to another matter.

- **Previous**. Before our interlocutor finishes the sentence, we are applying prejudices and beliefs.

- **Selective**. We focus only on what interests us.

- **Active**. We try to understand everything that is being said and, if we do not understand something, we ask or paraphrase for clarification.

- **Empathetic**. We try to understand how the interlocutor feels.

- **Egoless**. It is almost an act of love, in which we give ourselves body and soul to understand and connect emotionally with our interlocutor, forgetting ourselves. It is the most perfect listening there is.

— We have concluded by presenting the distinction between **empathic** listening and **sympathetic** listening.

The Ladder of Inference

If you remember the definitions from the first chapter, I introduced the definition of "Mental Models" as the set of beliefs that determines how we act. The Ladder of Inference is a model that explains the mental model that people follow when observing a situation, explaining when they draw their own conclusions and how they act. It was developed by the American psychologist Chris Argyris in 1985.

The phases are represented in a staircase, where the steps cover the different stages that lead to action:

- The **first** step is the bottom, and it is occupied by the **observed data** and **facts**.

- The **second** step is occupied by the **selection of observed data**. We tend to focus only on what interests us, so we omit the pieces of data that are less relevant to us.

- The **third** step **adds meaning, that is**, **interprets** the selected data, from a personal and cultural perspective: What is it? Why does it happen?

- In the **fourth** step, **assumptions are made** (we establish **causal relationships**) based on the meaning added on the previous step.

- In the **fifth** step, **conclusions are drawn** (**the causes are attributed**) based on the previous assumptions, which become "the truth" for us.

- In the **sixth** step, **beliefs are adopted** (**we generalize**) based on the conclusions obtained. These beliefs or generalizations give rise to emotions, preparing us for further action.

- Finally, we reach the **seventh** and last step, where **actions are carried out** based on the beliefs adopted.

This way of processing information can be disastrous when wrong conclusions are reached that lead to inappropriate actions. For example, in the movie *I Robot*, in it there's a scene where a robot runs down the street with a purse in hand that goes towards a woman who puts her hands to her throat.

- First step, facts of reality: The protagonist of the film, Will Smith, who plays the role of a police officer, observes this fact.

- Second step, data selection: The police officer selects the pieces of data that there is a robot running with a purse, and that a lady is screaming.

- Third step, data interpretation. The police officer adds the idea that it is very awkward for a robot to run around with a purse in hand.

- Fourth step, assumptions. Will Smith establishes the causal relationship that the lady screams because her purse has disappeared.

- Fifth step, conclusions. The policeman concludes that the robot has stolen the lady's purse and is on the run.

- Sixth step, adoption of beliefs. Will Smith generalizes and adopts the belief that robots, despite having the three laws of robotics, are capable of stealing, and in fact this one has stolen the lady's purse.

- Seventh step, execution of actions. The police officer, on the last step, decides to start a chase to recover the lady's purse. The scene ends with Will Smith rolling on the ground and throwing the robot, in front of the astonished eyes of the lady, who was asthmatic, and was waiting for her domestic robot to bring her the asthma inhaler.

In this example, if the police officer had observed objectively, he would have noticed that the robot was heading toward the lady, so it made no sense that it had stolen her purse. And, if he had continued observing, he would have realized that the lady was not yelling at the theft of her purse, but that she was telling the robot that she was at the bus stop, and that this was where the robot should take her purse. Therefore, a coach should train not to apply filters, and analyze the data in an aseptic and objective way, thus avoiding reaching false conclusions.

Antonio Montes Orozco

My advice is to always infer in the most **charitable** possible way.

HOW TO GET UP AND DOWN THE LADDER OF INFERENCE

The challenge as a coach is to stop interpreting in order to ask and listen. A first way to use the ladder would be to go down from the top step (the action), to the bottom step (the data and objective facts), going through the middle steps, until you discover what caused the action. I clarify it with an example:

If that greeting that X didn't give me the other day is interpreted as contempt, my reaction will be one of anger and misunderstanding. If, instead of settling for that, I ask X why he didn't reply to my greeting the other day, I may be surprised with his explanation: "My glasses have broken and without them I can't see well, so excuse me. I was afraid of responding incorrectly to the greetings, since I couldn't see and recognize the people, so I was walking looking at the ground so as not to meet anyone."

When we see that the judgments have appeared too soon, it is time to go back down to the first step. The objective piece of data is that X hasn't responded to my greeting. Possible interpretations: X hasn't noticed, X hasn't seen me, or X deliberately hasn't answered me. Therefore, it is time to collect more data and ask X directly. Trying to infer without having enough data is not recommended, as it can lead us to multiple embarrassing situations in life.

In this way we're aware of the steps we're taking; what data and facts we have; we realize when we're interpreting, when we're assuming, and what beliefs we're adopting. This awareness strengthens our communication with the team, since we make our perspective known; it leads us to know that of others; and it leads us to gather more information if necessary.

Next time you give a talk and see a colleague yawning, don't venture to think that you are boring them: remember the Ladder of Inference and think that there are many options and that you are missing data. For example, they may have had a bad night. Ask them instead.

DO NOT CONFUSE DATA WITH JUDGMENT

And there is still another detail that I would like to talk about, and that is the fact that, in our society, we often confuse objective data and facts with judgments and opinions. An objective piece of data is "John is seventy-four inches tall". One judgment, however, is "John is tall".

For example, if, at the end of a Sprint, the team sadly sees that they haven't had time to finalize the committed user stories because these were badly estimated, to accuse the Product Owner of being irresponsible or having the Product Backlog little refined, is a judgment. The objective piece of data is not that the Product Owner is irresponsible but that the end of the Sprint has not been reached because the user stories were poorly estimated. Delving into the objective data, the team will realize that it is necessary to refine the user stories, to be clear about their scope, and to be able to estimate them better. It is precisely the team that has to dedicate time to refining the tasks, since they are the ones who have to validate that the DoR (Definition of Ready) is met, to understand its scope and dependencies, and to be able to estimate them properly.

Mixing facts with opinions produces the following effects:

- **It distorts communication**. We've seen that the starting point on the Ladder of Inference is the observed objective facts, and considering judgments as observed objective facts distorts the whole set.

- **It leads us to think that our perception is the reality and to impose our point of view as the truth**. The truth is the objective facts, not our opinions and judgments. Therefore we are taking as "true" something totally debatable. Continuing with the example of the team that does not finish the committed tasks, the truth is that the committed tasks have not been carried out due to a bad estimate, not because the Product Owner is irresponsible.

- **Other points of view are annulled**. We've seen that the Ladder of Inference begins with facts and data, which are the "truth", and then making judgments and opinions. If we treat judgments from the beginning as if they were data, we leave no room to infer, thus nullifying other points of view. Let's remember that this could lead us to avoid everyone's participation and therefore not having the full team's commitment.

- **It is a hidden aggression**. If we return to the example of the Product Owner who is crossed out as irresponsibl, as an objective starting point, we are avoiding that there is another interlocutor with another opinion. We lack the opinion of the Product Owner himself, who is not present, or any other colleague who does not see the situation in the same way. Note that this aggression could lead to a lack of confidence, and a lack of confidence would lead to a lack of involvement, and therefore a lack of commitment.

THE TWELVE OBSTACLES TO COMMUNICATION

Before I list the twelve obstacles to communication, let me remind you of Stephen Covey's principle, which goes like this: "Without involvement there is no commitment". In communication we seek the commitment of the team or the interlocutor in front of us. Therefore, anything that leads us to lack of participation will eliminate our commitment. In the same way, I remind you that the lack of trust leads us to not participate, and therefore to a lack of commitment, as Patrick Lencioni teaches us (seen in the chapter on trust).

Record in your mind these twelve practices that can hinder the communication:

- **Do not order or demand**. An order eliminates involvement, and therefore commitment.

- **Do not threaten or warn**. A threat is an aggression that breaks trust, and a lack of trust leads to a lack of involvement, and without involvement there is no commitment.

- **Do not lecture**. Lecture is an aggression, because it puts us above the interlocutor, and that eliminates trust, leading to a lack of involvement, and therefore a lack of commitment.

- **Do not advise**. Advice is a solution to the problem that comes to us from outside, so we have not participated in it, and therefore we have not committed to it. For this reason coaches are not advisers.

- **Do not give lessons**. We draw on our experience to tell our interlocutor what is good or bad. A lesson is a form of aggression, where we manifest our superiority to the interlocutor. That eliminates trust, destroying participation, and therefore commitment.

- **Do not judge or criticize**. Being judged or criticized is an aggression that eliminates our confidence. Without trust we stop participating and without participation there is no commitment.

- **Do not flatter nor compliment**. Flattery could lead us to **sympathetic listening** and, if you remember when I explained it, this listening leads us to lose objectivity, because we accept everything our interlocutor tells us. It is a listening in which we will not be able to help anything at all.

- **Do not humiliate, ridicule, nor label**. It is an aggression, apart from a lack of respect, that leads to eliminating the interlocutor's trust toward us. At this point, you can imagine that this attitude will stop the commitment of our interlocutor.

- **Do not interpret nor diagnose**. It has to do with "reading the mind" of our interlocutor and, apart from being irrational to try to "read the mind", it is extremely irritating, because we are doing previous listening and filtering, moving away from the empathic egoless listening. Let's remember the Ladder of Inference: let's focus on objective data and facts, without applying filters.

- **Do not comfort**. It is a way of telling our interlocutor that what is happening to them is unimportant. It is extremely irritating and is linked to previous listening, distancing us from empathic, egoless listening.

- **Do not question**. Questioning what the interlocutor tells us is a sign of lack of trust, and indirectly an aggression, so we will eliminate their participation, and as a consequence their commitment.

- **Do not misrepresent, joke, nor use sarcasm**. It is an aggression and a lack of respect that eliminates trust.

SUMMARY

— The Ladder of Inference is a model that explains the phases that people follow when observing a situation, describing when they draw their own conclusions and how they act. The steps are:

- Observation of data and facts

- Data selection

- Data interpretation

- Establishment of assumptions

- Conclusions Obtention (I advise you to be **charitable** at this step).

- Adoption of beliefs

- Execution of acts

— Do not confuse data with judgment, as it is a hidden aggression that can lead to a lack of trust, a lack of participation, and as a consequence a lack of commitment.

— Lastly, we've seen the twelve enemies of communication, which lead us to make the interlocutor lose trust in us or feel attacked, ceasing to participate, and therefore ceasing to commit:

- Ordering or demanding

- Threatening or warning

- Lecturing

- Advising

- Giving lessons

- Judging or criticizing

- Flattering or complimenting

- Humiliating, ridiculing or labeling

- Interpreting or diagnosing

- Comforting

- Questioning

- Misrepresenting, joking, or using sarcasm

Nonviolent Communication

Nonviolent Communication (**NVC** from now on) is a model developed in the '60s by Marshall Rosenberg, an American psychologist who has authored numerous books such as *Nonviolent Communication*. This model seeks for people to communicate with each other with empathy and effectiveness, emphasizing the importance of clearly expressing observations, feelings, and needs so as to avoid violent language that judges and labels the interlocutors or third parties. We've already seen in the previous chapter that every aggression breaks communication.

Nonviolent Communication is also called "empathic communication" or "compassionate communication". It considers that all actions are originated in an attempt to satisfy needs (desires or goals), but that it is preferable to channel in a healthy and compassionate way, avoiding the use of fear, guilt, shame, accusation, and threats.

The NVC's ideal is that one's needs are not satisfied at the cost of frustrating the interlocutor's needs. For this, it is essential to express yourself without criticism or judgment about what is right or wrong. Instead, the focus is on expressing feelings and desires. The two key ideas that Rosenberg's model revolves around are the following:

- Our natural tendency is to feel satisfied when we give and receive something in solidarity.

- The human being has a natural tendency to compassion.

DISTINCTION BETWEEN "BEING" AND "DOING"

It is important to distinguish between "being" and "doing". The "being" identifies us as persons, while the "doing" is the result of our actions. When we see something that we do not like, we must focus on the "doing" of our interlocutor, because the "doing" always allows improvement. If we focus on the "being", we are orally attacking our interlocutor, creating mistrust and cutting off communication.

The fact that I make a mistake opens the possibility for me to learn from my "doing," and cause me to incorporate new strategies into my knowledge. But if the mistake is translated with the meaning that I am useless, or a disaster, or a bad professional, it is a sterile label that attacks us and that is useless.

In conclusion, remember to make requests for improvement to the "doing," and not to the "being". You'll avoid verbal attacks and open up new communication possibilities.

Antonio Montes Orozco

THE NVC MODEL TO ORDER

NVC consists of the following four steps:

1. Observing the objective **data** and **facts** of a given situation. Remember not to confuse objective facts and data with judgments or opinions.

2. Investigating **our emotions**: "Do we feel angry, offended, scared, happy, etc.?"

3. Identifying which of **our needs**, **wants,** or **goals** are related to the emotions we have discovered. Finding the genuine need and expressing it calmly and politely.

4. Making a **request** aimed at trying to meet the identified need.

For example, in the first step a mother observes that her daughter's clothes are lying on the floor of the room. Investigating her emotions, in the second step, she realizes that the disorder bothers her. Researching her needs in step three, she realizes that she needs to get her house tidy. By joining the first three steps, the mother can state:

"Sophie, it bothers me to see a shirt of yours on the sofa in the living room, because I like to see all the rooms in the house tidy."

Then the mother undertakes the fourth and final step, which consists of making a request:

"Sophie, could you pick up your shirt and take it to the laundry basket, please?"

In this way, there has been no aggression. Unfortunately, many families tend to label and judge, thus cutting off communication. See how different it would be to attack with labels and threats:

"Sophie, you are a *mess*! You've left your clothes lying around the house again! Immediately pick up your clothes or I'll punish you!"

The label *mess* is a verbal aggression and can also undermine the daughter's self-esteem. And on top of that, the petition ends with an imperative order and a threat: another verbal aggression. Thus there can be no healthy communication.

The same would apply in labor relations. The NVC way of raising needs and making requests is very powerful, and it helps a lot to preserve trust.

THE NVC MODEL TO OFFER

In the same way, this model is applied when offering help and meeting the needs of others. It is about extracting those four steps in others, connecting to first perceive what they observe, secondly perceive what they feel, thirdly listen to what they need, and finishing listening to their specific request, which will enrich their lives.

The essence of the NVC is in the awareness that we have of the four steps that we have seen. With practice, we will internalize Powerful Questions to extract the information at each step. Here's a graphic example: The quality manager states that the code generated by our team is useless. By asking questions, we can get the interlocutor to think about the four steps.

"The code you made is worthless," comments the Quality Manager. He does not have to know the NVC, and begins by labeling and attacking, but the Scrum Master understands that people do not know how to communicate, and ignores this comment, trying to investigate further, looking for the objective data. Scrum Masters require a lot of Temperance and self-control.

"Could you tell me which part isn't worth it, please?" answers the Scrum Master.

"You have performed operations on the graphic screens." This is the first objective piece of data that the Scrum Master perceives.

"What I'm getting at is that we've broken the Model-View-Controller philosophy. Is that what you mean?" The Scrum Master, paraphrasing, asks to make sure she understands what the problem is.

"Yes. There are a lot of programmers touching that code, and I don't want it to become unmaintainable in the future." The Quality Manager has expressed his emotions: he is afraid that the code will deteriorate. He also hints at his need, but it must be confirmed.

"What I understand is that you're thinking about the future of the application, and it causes you concern that the design patterns are broken, as it would make it difficult to maintain it. Is that true?" asks The Scrum Master.

"Yeah, that's it!"

"Is there anything else to fix? Any bug?"

"No, the operation is fine."

"So what can we do to get your approval of the code?"

"That you decouple the View from the Model and you do not enter calculations in the data presentation windows."

"Understood. We'll create a user story to refactor the code, and prioritize it to fit into the next Sprint. Of course, we will maintain the current behavior, so as not to break anything."

"That would be great," says the Quality Manager enthusiastically.

"Well, we will do it in the next Sprint!"

They both shake hands, very satisfied.

In this example we see that, by inquiring, there was only an error in form and not in substance, since the application was working well. The Scrum Master has shown her Temperance in the face of the Quality Manager's attack, since she knows perfectly that "being" is not the same as "doing", and, compassionately, she understands that it cannot be claimed that everyone knows the NVC and is an expert at communicating.

I encourage you to train yourself to use this model in all facets of your life. You will see the results very soon, and you will save yourself a lot of trouble.

DISTINCTION: GENEROSITY TO GIVE AND RECEIVE

We tend to understand generosity as how detached we are when it comes to giving. What's more, socially it looks good for a generous person to be sparing when it comes to accepting offers. But note that this throws relationships out of balance. Therefore, I propose to extend the concept of generosity to offer and to receive favors. In this way, we are generous when offering, but we let our interlocutor return the favor, being generous when receiving, thus balancing the relationship.

EFFECTIVE CONVERSATIONS

From Nonviolent Communication we have learned four steps that we have to cover in order to reach a healthy agreement. The usual thing is that, in the conversations, needs are transmitted by both parties, so we'll have to be aware of our own needs and also those of our interlocutor, covering the four steps for both. But it is difficult to get it right the first time if we don't come prepared. I propose the following script to prepare an effective conversation:

1) Setting the **context**. The moment, the place, how am I? How is my interlocutor?

2) Being clear about the **concern** that originates the conversation. What do I want this conversation for?

3) Making a list of **facts** and **pieces of data**: Remember not to confuse objective facts and pieces of data with judgments and opinions. They must be presented in a clear and concise way: "I have seen …"; "I observe that …"

4) Identifying **interpretations/emotions**: "When you do this, I think that…" / "When this happens, I feel that…" / "How do you see it?" / "What do you feel when…?" An egoless, empathic listening is necessary to identify the interpretations and emotions of our interlocutor.

5) Specifying my **needs** and those of my interlocutor: "What I need is…" / "I understand that what you need is…"

6) **Commitment to the future**. A request, an agreement, future actions…

When a conversation takes place, it must be taken into account whether the trend is competitive (for example, the one we have with a seller who offers us their product) or collaborative (the one we may have with work colleagues).

In a competitive conversation the relationship is punctual and there is little transparency. On the contrary, in a collaborative conversation the relationship is continuous over time, and there is a lot of information transparency.

As coaches, we should try to have collaborative conversations, as they are more productive. To do this, the coach tries to discover the complementary needs of both parties, and thus enter into a collaborative conversation.

SUMMARY

— Nonviolent Communication (NVC) is a model that Marshall Rosenberg created in the 1960s. It consists of applying the following four steps in conversations where there are requests and offers:

    1. Observing the **data** and objective facts of a given situation.

    2. Investigating our **emotions** or those of our interlocutor, based on the facts and data that are presented.

    3. Identifying what our **needs** (desires, goals) or those of our interlocutor are.

4. Making a **request** aimed at trying to achieve the identified need or make an **offer** that fulfills the need of our interlocutor.

— We've seen the distinction applied to generosity, expanding this concept both to offer our help and to receive it, thus balancing our relationships.

— We've also learned the distinction between "being" and "doing", to avoid verbal aggression to our interlocutor, and focus only on their actions.

— Finally, I've proposed a script to prepare the conversations, so that they are effective:

1) Setting the **context**.

2) Being clear about the **concern** that the conversation causes.

3) Making a list of the objective **pieces of data** and **facts**.

4) Investigating my **emotions** and **interpretations** and those of my interlocutor.

5) Specifying my **needs** and those of my interlocutor.

6) Seeking future commitment.

— As a reading for this chapter, I recommend *Nonviolent Communication* by Marshall Rosenberg.

Feedback

The feedback consists of communicating to our interlocutor what their "doing" is like, to learn from mistakes and improve, or, if the feedback is positive, simply to reinforce their current actions. According to the purpose of the feedback we have the following distinctions:

DISTINCTIONS FOR FEEDBACK

- **Valuable feedback**. It is the one that serves us, the one that takes us out of the box. For example, this type belongs to the feedback that the Product Owner gives us when we show them the work done in the *Sprint Review* meeting.

- **Recognition feedback**. In it we talk about the "being" and the "doing", and it serves to make it clear to our interlocutor which actions are welcome and must be maintained.

- **Feedback for learning** (**mirror feedback**). We do not talk about what our interlocutor "is", but about their "doing", and how what they do impacts me. For this reason, it is always done in the first person: "What I think about what you do..." Feedback is often associated with the idea of a mirror in which we look at ourselves, and hence it is also called "mirror feedback".

- **Feedforward**. It is a new concept that has been invented to designate a future-oriented feedback, to agree on concrete improvement actions. It is to negotiate needs and to generate new commitments in the future, so that feedforward empowers our interlocutor.

PROCEDURE TO GIVE FEEDBACK

All feedback is a valuable gift, as it makes our interlocutor react, either to improve, or to confirm that they are on the right track. But you cannot give feedback at any time, you have to ask permission to give it. And we have to be open to being told no.

Outlined below are the seven steps to give feedback:

1. Asking yourself **what** we are going to give it **for**.

2. Asking **permission** and creating **context**: "I would like to give you feedback: is it a good time now?"

3. Keeping in mind that it is a **gift** and that it is only our opinion: "It is only my opinion, and I would like to give it to you, in case it serves you."

4. **Giving our opinion** on what our interlocutor does, not on what they are: "When I see that... I think..." It is important to focus on objective facts and data, so we must avoid expressions such as "always" or "never". It is better to replace it

with "sometimes". Remember that if we are giving a feedforward, we must talk about the future more than the past.

5. Performing **egoless empathic listening**, so we attend to the emotions and needs of our interlocutor as well as our own. From there, offers, requests, and future commitments arise.

6. **Leaving space** for our interlocutor to decide what to do with our feedback: "I hope it helps you."

7. **Being grateful** for the feedback received: "Thank you." On this last step, we cannot expect our interlocutor to thank us: remember that, in this Society, we are not taught to listen or communicate efficiently. We are coaches and we train for it, but we cannot demand this skill from everyone. However, if we're given feedback, let's remember that it is a gift, and that we should be grateful for it.

If we are given feedback badly, losing objectivity and making judgments, we can consider giving feedback on the feedback received.

POWERFUL QUESTIONS TO GIVE FEEDFORWARD

Here you have some Powerful Questions to give feedforward and look to the future:

"If you had to do it again, what would you change?"

"What are you going to do differently next time?"

"What strategies will you apply to overcome the obstacles that may arise?"

"After this conversation, what are you going to put into practice in the future?"

"In what situations could you apply what we have talked about?"

"What requests or offers could you make for…?"

"What commitments do you want to make in relation to the actions you have identified?"

SUMMARY

— The feedback consists of communicating to our interlocutor how their "doing" is.

— We've seen some distinctions associated with feedback: valuable feedback, recognition feedback, feedback for learning, and feedforward.

— We've also seen the steps that are followed to give our feedback:

> 1) What we are going to give it for.
>
> 2) Asking for permission and creating context.

3) Remembering that it is a gift.

4) Giving our opinion on the doing of the interlocutor.

5) Egoless empathic listening. Offers, requests, and commitments to future arise.

6) Leaving space for our interlocutor to decide what to do with our feedback.

7) Thanking for the feedback received.

— Finally, I've proposed to you some Powerful Questions to give feedforward.

Observer OSAR Model

The OSAR model is an acronym that stands for **O**bserver, **S**ystem, **A**ction, and **R**esult. It is one of the fundamental models used in Coaching to make changes that seek improvement, and it was created by Rafael Echeverría, a Chilean doctor of philosophy and president of the Newfield Group. These improvement changes can be applied to both professional life and personal life.

In this model, the results that we obtain are produced by actions performed by an observer in a specific system. The observer is really us, and we are the ones who evaluate the efficacy of the results. The important thing is the results, not the intentions. These results are the criteria that should motivate us to act, so resignation is the greatest enemy of improvement. If the results are as desired, the process ends. On the contrary, if the results are not the desired ones, the first level of learning consists of **modifying the way of acting** and checking if the desired result is achieved.

If, after changing the way of acting, the goal is achieved, the process ends, and the **Learning** that we have achieved is said to be of **First Order**. This is the learning that we are traditionally taught. Observation is done on **WHAT**. The questions associated with first-order learning are of the form: "What are you going to do?" "What did you do in other occasions?" "What did you do that you have to stop doing?" "What didn't you do that you have to do?"

But, if modifying the way of acting does not achieve the desired result, we can focus on the next level of learning, which consists of **modifying the way of observing**. If we focus on the observer, we put the goal aside and observe what is happening to the observer, paying attention to what is preventing them from moving forward. This is what **Second Order Learning** consists of: observation is made on the **WHO**. The questions associated with second order learning are of the form: "Who are you being?" "Who it is for?" "What information does it give you?" A typical example of Second Order Learning is modifying the metrics or evaluation criteria used.

If the expected result is still not achieved, we advance to the next level of learning, which consists of **changing the beliefs of the observer**. If the observer, in order to advance, needs to change deep beliefs that modify their way of being in the world, they need **Transformational Learning**: the observation is carried out on **WHO IN RELATION TO**. After transformational learning, we are no longer what we were, as we have transformed our deepest beliefs. The questions associated with transformational learning are of the form: "How does it impact your environment?" "Who do we want to be as a team?" For example, in Agile, the beliefs are to empower the team so that all team members participate in decisions and can commit. Therefore, project managers and teams need to transform to embrace the new belief that empowering a team, and giving it full trust, is the way to achieve a committed and high-performing team.

Finally, if after acting on the observer and the actions we still do not achieve the expected result, we have to **change the system**. This is what I call **Learning of Base**. For example, the Agile spirit has caused the company hierarchies to be flattened, eliminating bosses in favor of "roles".

DISTINCTIONS FOR TYPES OF LEARNING

We've learned new distinctions to apply to the word learning:

- **First Order Learning,** which is the derivative of changing the way of acting. It is the traditional way in which we have understood learning.

- **Second Order Learning,** which is the derivative of changing the way of observing. For example, changing a metric or evaluation criteria.

- **Transformational Learning,** which is the derivative of changing the beliefs of the observer. For example, incorporating the beliefs of Agilism.

- **Learning of Base**, which is the derivative of changing the system itself. For example flattening hierarchies in the company.

AGILE OBSERVER

And now that I have presented the OSAR model, where the observer has a preponderant position, what is an Agile observer like? We see that we will have to transform ourselves to:

- Change our relationships with our colleagues.

- Change the way we listen and debate, and the way we understand and embrace discrepancies.

- Be able to show transparency and Humility.

- Find out that being generous and openly grateful is worth the effort.

- Convert feedback into "feedforward" on a regular basis, that is, use learning from the past to improve the future.

An Agilist transformation implies a profound cultural change, not just the mere practice of ceremonies. Agilism extends to the cognitive, personal, professional, social levels, and, finally, to the level of change.

SUMMARY

— **OSAR** (**O**bserver, **S**ystem, **A**ction, **R**esult) is a model that allows us to visualize the process that is carried out in a system, to generate results. There are different levels of learning:

- Learning the capacity for action (**First Order**). It occurs when we learn to perform new actions, and that allows us to obtain new results.

- Learning the ability to observe (**Second Order**). It occurs when we change some limiting thoughts or judgments, and that expands our possibilities of action. For example, modifying the metrics or the evaluation criteria.

- Learning beliefs (**Transformational**). It occurs when we transform ingrained beliefs and assumptions, thus changing the way we are in the world. For example, incorporating the Agile philosophy into our beliefs.

- Learning at the **Base**. It occurs when we transform the system itself, changing the base environment that surrounds us. For example, to flatten hierarchies in the company.

— Finally, we've seen the transformational levels of the Agile observer: cognitive, personal, professional, social, and attitude towards change.

Methodologies to Generate Action Plans

SMART CHALLENGES

Through questions and egoless empathic listening we have understood what our interlocutor needs, and we have felt their emotions, arriving at the proposal to undertake a challenge and activate an improvement plan. In order not to lose focus, we reuse the acronym **SMART** that Agilism teaches us. This acronym will always remind us of how those challenges that we set ourselves should be, just as it reminds us of how the *User Stories* of the *Product Backlog* should be:

- **Specific**. The human being, to undertake an action plan, needs the goal to be very specific, in order to be able to concentrate on it and put all their efforts into achieving it. We have to answer the following questions:

> "How am I going to achieve what I want to achieve?"
>
> "What specific actions am I going to do?"
>
> "When am I going to do them?"
>
> "Whom should I involve?"
>
> "What do I need to learn?"
>
> "Whom can I rely on?"

"How will I know that I am getting it?"

- **Measurable**. It is very important that the challenge is measurable and verifiable. This quality is closely related to the first one, that is, to being specific, because precisely that specificity will lead us to verify the degree of achievement of the challenge posed.

- **Achievable** by oneself. If we set ourselves a challenge in which we depend on others to achieve it, we are sold. The same applies to team challenges: the team must be able to meet the challenge without external dependencies.

- **Relevant**. The challenge must be relevant to ourselves and to the Organization. In Agile terms: it has to add value.

- **Time** bounded. If we do not limit the challenge in time, we won't feel the pressure of time that is running out, and we won't dedicate efforts to achieve the challenge that we've set ourselves. This time constraint is closely related to the property of being Measurable, since we know that, when the time is up, one hundred percent of the challenge must have been achieved.

It is interesting to apply the SMART quality of user stories to the improvement challenges that we propose ourselves. That brings us to the next distinction.

DISTINCTION: "BEING AGILIST" AND "DOING AGILISM"

"Doing Agilism" is to perform the typical Agile ceremonies and rituals (Daily, Sprint Planning, Sprint Review, Retrospective, etc.), putting user stories on a panel, estimating with Scrum Poker cards, etc.

"Being an Agilist" is a lifestyle, a way of being that enriches ourselves and the company, seeking value in everything we do, prioritizing our personal tasks to maximize it, and always being willing to improve.

METHODOLOGY TO ACHIEVE THE CHALLENGE

Once we have decided to go for a challenge, it is achieved in the same way in which user stories are finished in Sprints:

1) **The action plan is set**, which must be SMART, in the same way that the user stories that enter the Sprint are set.

2) Every day we **evaluate** the progress of the achievement of the challenge, just as the team celebrates the *Daily* every day to synchronize.

3) When the deadline expires, the result is **reviewed**, just like the *Sprint Review* meeting is held in Agile.

4) And finally, in the same way that the *Sprint Retrospective* meeting is held in Agilism, the team (or we individually) sets

new challenges to improving continuously, returning to step 1.

Notice that over and over again we find that "being an Agilist" is a way of life that we apply in all facets of our day. Who would have told us that the cyclical process that is used to develop software products in Agile, is just the cyclical process that is used in Continuous Improvement.

Once I have explained how the Continuous Improvement process is carried out, there remains a small detail: how is the action plan established? It is time to introduce you to the GROW methodology to create action plans.

GROW METHODOLOGY

The GROW methodology for generating action plans was created by Alexander Graham and Sir John Whitmore in the 1980s. It is an acronym that comes from the words **Goal**, **Reality**, **Options**, and **Will**. It consists of the following steps:

1) **Setting the goal**. In this first step our interlocutor defines and establishes the goal to be achieved. For this step we can use the Powerful Questions: "What is your goal?" "What would you like to achieve?"

2) **Examining Reality**. In this second step, the current situation of our interlocutor is examined and described, evaluating what

they lack to achieve their goal. In this step we can ask questions such as, "In what situation are you now?" or, "What would you need to get there?"

3) **Analyzing Options**. In this third step, we analyze the options and possibilities that are presented to our interlocutor to overcome the limitations that prevent them from achieving their goal. I propose the following questions: "What alternatives do you have?" or, "How could you get it?"

4) **Generating a plan**. In this fourth and final step our interlocutor shows their willingness and commitment to reach their goal with a detailed plan that is **SMART** (Acronym seen above for specific, measurable, achievable, relevant, and time-bounded goals). In this last step we can use the Powerful Questions "What are you going to do?" "How are you going to check that you are doing it?" "What do you need to do it?" "How long do you give yourself to get it?"

FCA METHODOLOGY

We do not always have time to apply GROW calmly, and we have to get more to the point. Imagine a *Retrospective* meeting where many topics come up and the team wants to take action on each of them, with little time left to finish the meeting. Now is the time to use a lighter method, like the one that I call **FCA**, an acronym that comes from **F**acts, **C**auses, and **A**ctions. This methodology consists of just three steps:

1) **Presenting the data and facts**. Remember not to confuse objective facts and data with judgments and opinions.

2) **Determining the causes** that have led to the facts and data listed in the previous step.

3) **Proposing actions** that help to achieve the goal. Remember that the agreed actions have to be **SMART**.

RECURRING PROBLEMS

If the actions do not take effect on a recurring basis, and the same problems always appear in *Retrospectives*, it's time to remember the OSAR model that we saw in the previous chapter. The learning that we've had so far has been of First Order, as we've focused only on modifying the way of acting. It is time to modify the way of observing, to obtain a Second Order learning.

SUMMARY

- We've seen the acronym SMART, which helps us define the improvement actions that we consider: specific, measurable, achievable, relevant, and time-bounded.

- We've learned the distinction between "Being Agile" and "Doing Agile", as an attitude of life as contraposition of the mere performance of rituals.

- We've also learned that the improvement process, once an action has been set, is very similar to the Agile iterative process: setting the action plan, periodically evaluating the progress of the plan, analyzing the final result, and proposing new challenges.

- Then we've seen two methodologies to generate action plans: the **GROW** (goal, reality, options, and will) and the lighter **FCA** (facts, causes, and actions).

- We've also linked the recurring problems with the OSAR model, to remind us to change the observer when the problems have not finished being solved and appear repeatedly.

- As a bibliography, you can read John Whitmore's own book, *Coaching for Performance*, written in 1992.

Questions

We've seen that questions are the tool that the coach uses to make us reflect and motivate us to action. Powerful Questions are thought-provoking and insightful. The questions can be of many types, depending on the intention they contain.

- **Closed** questions: questions that can only have a yes or a no answer, which is why they are poor when it comes to inviting reflection. For example: "Did you like the end of Sprint?"

- **Open** questions: questions that await an explanation. These questions invite more reflection than the closed ones to the reflection. For example, "What did you think of this Sprint?" These questions belong to the group of Powerful Questions.

- Questions to the **past** / **present** / **future**: We learn from the past, we are in the present, and in the future the improvement actions to which we commit ourselves will take place. For example, we ask the past: "How did you feel at that moment?" Now we ask the present: "How does this make you feel?" And now we ask the future, to seek compromise: "What are you going to do to avoid this situation next time?" The questions to the past/present/future belong to the group of Powerful Questions.

- **Chained** questions: These are the questions that chain several ideas, which may in the end confuse our interlocutor. For example: "What did you think of the end of the sprint, when from the beginning you saw that you were delayed, and in the middle you received new user stories, and, now that we are here, don't you fancy a coffee?" Our interlocutor is already thinking about a delicious coffee and a break from our chained questions.

- **Remedy** question. It's the one that manipulates, already showing a solution, moving away from the philosophy of Coaching, where the coach does not advise but helps to explore. For example: "What do you think if you check daily if your plan is going well?" If the coach detects that the possibility of review has not yet been explored, an open question that invites reflection is better: "How are you going to be sure that your plan is working?"

- **Formula** question. In this type of question a methodology is being proposed, so it is a form of manipulation. Everything that is manipulation is far from Coaching, since Coaching motivates us and seeks our commitment, being clear that our commitment will come from our personal reflection. For example: "What do you think about setting your goal, reflecting on your current situation, thinking about your options, and committing to an action?" It would be much more honest to go exploring with open questions like "What is your objective?" Then asking, "What situation are you currently in?" You can continue like this: "What options do you currently have?" To end with the Powerful Question: "What are you going to do?"

- Question that seeks **justifications** with the "why?". This question lends itself a lot to our interlocutor feeling cornered and answering us with an elusive justification. Therefore these questions are discouraged.

- Question that seeks **intentions** with the "what for?". This question is very powerful and encourages us to explore the intent behind the facts. Moreover, when misfortunes happen to us, it is much healthier to ask "what for?", since every misfortune has its good side and we can learn from every misfortune, than asking "why", which will sink us into sadness and despair.

Therefore a coach is trained to ask Powerful Questions, which are open, to seek the intentions of the interlocutor, and can be thrown into the past, present, or future.

SUMMARY

- Questions are the tool that the coach uses to make us reflect and motivate us to action.

- A coach is trained to ask Powerful Questions that are open, which seek intentions and can be thrown into the past, present or future.

- Avoid closed questions, chained questions, remedial questions, formula questions, and questions seeking justifications.

Antonio Montes Orozco

The Change of Beliefs

Beliefs are our interpretation, sculpted in the brain, of the world around us. Beliefs are changed through reflection and the practice of new actions, until incorporating them into our mental model. Therefore, to adopt a new belief it is necessary to learn.

Before continuing, I am going to present you a new distinction:

DISTINCTION: DEMAND VS. EXCELLENCE

The path of "demand" is the path where you seek to do things perfectly. Perfection does not exist, so its search becomes impossible, causing frustration in those who insist on following this path.

In contrast, we have the path of "excellence", where we seek Continuous Improvement, and the learning that making mistakes provides us. We assume that erring is human, and we see in each error a possibility of improvement. This practice, continued over time, leads us to self-esteem, satisfaction, and excellence.

Before continuing, let's review the beliefs that the Agile Coach (or Agilist Coach, as I like to call it) needs to have.

AGILIST COACH BELIEFS

I present to you some of the Agilist Coach's beliefs:

- **Respect** and **trust** facilitate team members' collaboration. Without respect trust is lost, and we have already seen that without trust there is no commitment.

- **We need others** to complete a task. We must be humble and recognize that we cannot do it alone. This society tends toward pride and self-sufficiency, despising teamwork.

- **Everything can be improved**, and you have to be open to self-criticism and get feedback in order to improve. Again we see how useful it is being humble.

- **Taking risks** increases team awareness. Error is a learning opportunity. You should never stop trying to improve for fear of error. Here I remember the slogan from my second book: "Eliminate fear from the equation." To be an Agilist you need to have a great deal of courage.

- **There is always room for improvement** (demand vs. excellence). We are not satisfied with going through the motions, but we seek excellence, as a result of seeing the error as an opportunity for improvement.

- The important thing is **delivering value**. That's why we prioritize tasks according to the value they add to the Business.

- The only thing that remains is **change**. The change allows us to adapt, and take advantage of the Business opportunities that are presented to us.

- Everything works better by **sharing solutions**. We eliminate interdepartmental compartments to make way for transparency, and generous sharing of knowledge.

ENEMIES OF CHANGE

Here are some positions in life that prevent us from changing:

- **Not admitting our ignorance**. Don't be afraid to say, "I do not know." Once again, we see how important it is for the Agile Coach to be humble and sincere.

- **Pretending to have everything clear, all the time**. We reject what we do not understand for fear of the unknown. Humility leads us to recognize what we don't know.

- **Judging everything, all the time**. It is easier to label a new methodology as useless than to confront what it can teach us. Labels are a way of justifying our inaction. Learning involves effort and an act of Humility, clashing with the pride and laxity that prevails in the twenty-first century society.

- **Thinking that, given who I am, I can't learn**. Again reactive and victim thinking, where, by labeling ourselves as useless,' we justify ourselves not to make an effort and learn.

- **Not giving authority to those who teach us**. The Agile Coach is our teacher. Through prejudice and labeling we remove authority from them, preventing them from enlightening us. One more form of justification for not reacting and learning.

- **Believing that having information is synonymous with "knowing how to do"**. Having read a book, a blog, or having a coffee conversation does not imply "knowing how to do." Know-how involves theory, lots of practice, and making mistakes. Only when we've accumulated a sufficient number of mistakes we'll begin to "know how to do".

- **Being afraid, uncomfortable with change**. Remember the slogan from my second book: Eliminate fear from the equation. With desire and effort, everything is possible. To be an Agilist, you need to have a high dose of courage.

- **Confusing what I know with what I am**. Not knowing a new way of working does not make us useless. Again labels and prejudices justify us not to fight.

- **Adopting a reactive attitude toward life**, instead of a proactive one. A proactive attitude is that of people responsible for their lives who know that they can improve and change, so they take charge of their existence, continually improving and achieving excellence. A reactive attitude is that of people who act as victims, ignoring that they can improve and change, so they tend to justify themselves to not acting, therefore stagnating in mediocrity.

Antonio Montes Orozco

In relation to this last point, I present to you a distinction on the attitude toward life.

DISTINCTION: VICTIM VS. RESPONSABLE

In relation to the attitude we take toward life, we find ourselves with the reactive position versus the proactive one. This distinction is very important because, honestly, I believe that it is impossible to improve with a reactive mindset. Agilism implies a very proactive attitude toward change. For this reason, it is important that the coach makes the team see the differences between victimizing language versus responsible one.

Here are some examples of reactive thoughts versus proactive ones:

"They don't understand me, there is no way with these people." Proactive thinking would be this: "I'm not explaining myself."

"I can't trust him, he gets lost all the time." And the proactive way: "I'll explain it to him again."

"I got soaked because it rains." Versus the proactive version: "I got soaked because I didn't grab the umbrella."

"I don't have time to start learning a new language. My time's all accounted for." Proactive version: "I'm going to reorganize myself to find time in my life and start learning a new language."

"They don't give me the resources to do what they ask me to do." And now the proactive version: "I'm going to specify what I need and then ask for it."

The victim perceives that their circle of influence is small, so they exempt responsibilities. Victim language is also known as "disempowered language." Responsible language is known as "empowered language."

Let's delve into the concept of assuming the role of victim. I am going to introduce you to the Nine Cognitive Distortions.

THE NINE COGNITIVE DISTORTIONS

Cognitive distortions are **irrational thoughts** that provoke negative feelings (anxiety, anger, depression). They constitute a fallacious way of reasoning. They transform reality and are opposed to any attempt at Continuous Improvement. If we want to enter a virtuous path of Continuous Improvement with the team, it is important that we detect these irrational ways of thinking in the team, in order to tackle them at the root. Some of the most common cognitive distortions are:

- **Emotional reasoning**. When we let our feelings guide our interpretation of reality, because we have the false belief that our emotions reflect reality. From what we've seen so far, this takes us away from objective data and facts. Some examples of emotional reasoning: "I feel incompetent, therefore I am incompetent." "I feel that way, then it has to be true."

- **Catastrophism**. When we focus on the worst possible outcome and see it as the most likely, without any reason to do so. For example, we turn a small headache into brain cancer.

- **Overgeneralization**. When we draw a general conclusion from a specific event that has happened to us. For example, if I'm having a bad day, my life is already a "dead end chaos". Another example: if a Sprint goes wrong because several colleagues have fallen ill, it does not mean that the delivery date will not be reached and that the project is "floored".

- **Dichotomous thinking**. When we see events or judge people in terms of all or nothing. For example, if this Sprint the Product Owner has not been able to maintain the Product Backlog because he's been assigned another project and he is saturated, we call him irresponsible, when recently he was a great professional.

- **Mind reading**. When we assume that we know what people think without having sufficient evidence of their true judgments or thoughts. For example, the boss places an order on a colleague and not on us. The irrational thought would be: "Sure, the boss doesn't like me. He thinks that I'm not working well enough, and so he puts me aside."

- **Labeling**. When we assign a name to something instead of objectively describing the behavior observed, both in others and in ourselves. For example, "I'm clumsy", "They're a mess", "He's boring".

- **Negative filtering**. When, in any situation, we focus exclusively on the negative details, thus perceiving that the whole situation is negative. For example, let's consider a student who takes a test of one hundred questions and, after completing it, he finds out that he's failed seven. He applies negative filtering and thinks he's going to suspend. As the exam results are published, he discovers that he's answered ninety-three questions correctly and that he therefore got an A.

- **Disqualification of the positive**. When we affirm that the positive things that we do or that others do are trivial, so we maintain a negative judgment. For example, we get a compliment at work for finishing a difficult user story well, and we think, "They want to look good, and nothing else."

- **Blaming**. We blame another person or ourselves for the problems, regardless of the causes of the problems and the people involved. An example of this irrational way of thinking would be: "If I hadn't been on vacation, the Sprint would have gone well. We have not finished because of me."

SUMMARY

— Beliefs are our interpretation of the world around us. Adopting a new belief requires learning.

— I've presented you with a new distinction: **demand vs. excellence**, so that we distinguish between the unhealthy search for perfection versus the path of Continuous Improvement.

— I've also shared the Agilist coach's beliefs with you:

    - Respect and trust facilitate collaboration of team members.

    - We need others to complete a task.

    - Everything can be improved.

    - Taking risks increases the team's knowledge.

    - There is always room for improvement (demand vs. excellence).

    - The important thing is to deliver value.

    - The only thing that remains is change.

    - Everything works better by sharing solutions.

— I've also introduced you to the enemies of change:

    - Not admitting our ignorance.

Antonio Montes Orozco

- Pretending to have everything clear, all the time.

- Judging everything, all the time.

- Thinking that, given who I am, I can't learn.

- Not giving authority to those who teach us.

- Believing that having information is synonymous with "knowing how to do".

- Being afraid of or uncomfortable with change.

- Confusing what I know with what I am.

- Adopting a reactive attitude towards life, instead of a proactive one.

— I've also presented the distinction between **victim** attitude vs. **responsible** attitude.

— To finish, I have presented you with the nine **Cognitive Distortions** that provoke irrational thoughts in us, leading us to suffer, to a depressive state, and a reactive attitude towards life:

- Emotional reasoning

- Catastrophism

- Overgeneralization

- Dichotomous thinking

- Mind reading

- Labeling

- Negative filtering

- Disqualification of the positive

- Blaming.

— As a bibliography for this chapter, I recommend my second book, *The Work Stress Cycle*.

Examples of Coaching Sessions

We are reaching the end of the road and we have learned a lot of theory. But mastering the technique of putting it into practice is not easy, so I propose two examples of what could be typical Coaching sessions.

THE IRASCIBLE PROGRAMMER

In this example of Coaching session, Robert, a Scrum Master, discovers in a *Retrospective* meeting that one of the programmers, William, is aggressively treating his colleagues, labeling their code as "botched". This, together with some comments that have reached Robert's ears, with complaints of the bad manners of the aforementioned programmer, predisposes him to have a Coaching session with William, to see what is happening and what is the origin of his attitude. Our Scrum Master is a professional, so he prepares the feedback session before having the meeting: he will give the programmer feedback to discover what leads him to be aggressive with his colleagues, since this could undermine trust inside the team, leading to disastrous consequences.

"Hello, Bill. I have summoned you to have a chat and give you feedback. Do I have your permission to give it to you?" asks

Robert, who knows that feedback requires the permission of our interlocutor.

"Yeah, come on, shoot," William replies.

"The other day, in the *Retro*, I saw you telling your coworkers that their code was botched. I would like to know how you see yourself on the team, and what led you to say that." Robert gets to the point. The best thing is to be direct and not beat around the bush, but always from the self, with objective data, without labeling and with respect.

"Ah, is it that? Well, in this team, except for those who program the services, the rest have no idea. What a bunch of useless programmers we have!"

Robert has to use all his Temperance and tell himself that others don't have to know how to carry on a conversation, so he begins to ask Powerful Questions with great patience.

"Could you explain to me what they have no idea about, please?" Robert asks, starting the ladder of inference from the first step and trying to find objective data.

"Well, they usually call our service modules from the graphic screens, bundling the code and making the application go very slow," William replies.

"What else do you observe?" Robert asks, inquiring.

"Well, I see they're also coupling the code." They aren't using interfaces, and that makes it so that any change involves changing a bunch of classes. There's a very high risk of introducing errors with any change," William answers.

"And how does that make you feel?" Robert is mentally reviewing the NVC. It is important to determine the data and the emotions that they cause, to later be able to specify needs.

"But are you a dumb or what, Rob?" What's that, how does it make me feel? Very angry indeed! What a shitty team!"

Robert observes with pity the amount of inferences that William makes, disrespecting and labeling his coworkers. But he wants to stay calm. He repeats to himself that he has to have Temperance and keeps asking, to confirm the emotions and the objective data and facts.

"I understand that your anger is due to the fact that the design patterns in the code have not been respected, apart from the fact that it is also being coupled, creating dependencies between classes, which would make its maintenance difficult. Is that so?"

"Sure, that would piss anyone off."

"I've also detected that this situation leads you to question the possibilities of this team." Robert has to inquire into William's needs.

"Of course. If the Top Management of this Company doesn't know how to hire good programmers, and it brings us these useless ones, we're going bad."

Now Robert sees the moment to turn feedback into feedforward.

"And how would you like them to be?" Robert asks.

"Well, more senior, and that at least they know about design patterns, and programming without coupling the code, so as not to destroy the application."

"If you had to hire them, what knowledge would you ask them to have?" Robert begins to be clear about William's needs and, through questions, is getting him to focus on his need, after having started from objective data and having specified what this data causes in his emotions.

"Well, knowing the patterns Model-View-Controller, Publisher & Subscriber, and Factory, and knowing the basic programming rules. You can't imagine the bungling I've discovered in the code."

"And where can such programmers be found?" Robert asks a Powerful Question to make William aware of the team's needs.

"I don't know. That's not my problem."

"And could something be done to get it out of the way?" Robert keeps on insisting with Powerful Questions.

"I guess I could give them a programming course. I don't see any other way to get something out of them."

"It would be very generous of you. What would you need to be able to give them a course?"

Antonio Montes Orozco

William already sees a solution, so now it's the time to facilitate his initiative. "Three days, a room with a projector, and lengthening the delivery time, because the course would stop us in our tracks with the project," says William.

"And do you see any way to give them the course without having to stop the project in its tracks?" Robert, apart from being a coach, is the Scrum Master of the team, and a pause in the rhythm has to be very justified.

"Well, I don't know. Instead of doing three sessions of five hours, which would take away three days of work, I can divide it into separate sessions of half an hour, distributed on alternate days. That would have little impact."

"And how would you verify that your teaching has penetrated the team?" Robert helps William set a SMART goal.

"Well, I guess we can do a code review session after the *Retro* meeting, or even during it."

"It sounds great to me, Bill. When do we start, and how do we notify it?"

"I suggest we start tomorrow, and tell the programmers about it right now, when we leave this room."

"I think it's great, Bill. What I've understood is that we leave it in about thirty sessions of half an hour, on alternate days, and starting tomorrow, we would finish the training in two months and little more, without stopping the rhythm. Is it right?"

"Yeah."

"Well, I reserve a room with a projector, for alternate days, for the next two months."

"Great, Rob! Thanks a lot!"

In this example we have reviewed the NVC (Nonviolent Communication), as Robert has helped William to review the four steps, to focus on data, see the emotions that caused him, find out his needs, and be able to translate it into an action plan. There Robert has also mixed GROW to investigate the possible options. We have also gone through the ladder of inference, discovering why William had the team labeled in such a derogatory way. And, since the solution to the problem went through an action plan, Robert made sure that it was SMART (specific, measurable, achievable, relevant and limited in time).

What Coaching gives us are tools and methodologies, which cannot always be applied in a purist way, but rather we have to pick up what we need as the conversation progresses. At no point has William felt psychoanalyzed, and the conversation has flowed productively. We've also seen the advantage of having Temperance and not getting carried away by labels and aggressive tones. As Robert hasn't said anything but has only asked, and it has been William who has said everything, in the end he has committed to teach his coworkers, to fill the gap in knowledge that he has detected.

Antonio Montes Orozco

THE DISTRACTED PROGRAMMER

In this Coaching session Robert, our beloved Scrum Master, notices that Caroline, a team programmer, has been late for *Daily Scrum* meetings for the last few weeks and is slowing down, spending too much time on the user stories that she undertakes, and failing to finish them. Her decline in performance is beginning to impact the team. Robert decides to have a Coaching session with her.

"Good morning, Carol. How do you feel?"

"Good, very good."

"I'm meeting you to give you feedback. Can you give me your permission?"

"Yeah, of course."

"This last week I've noticed that you were late for the *Dailies*. I've also noticed that you've assumed the implementation of a seemingly simple user story, and that you've been with it for quite a few days. Which leads me to wonder if you're okay. How do you feel?" Robert knows to get to the point but always presents the data and facts.

"Good, very good." This answer from Caroline doesn't fit the objective data, so Robert infers that there is something that worries the programmer. He's got to insist.

"How do you feel on the team?" asks Robert.

"Good, very good," Caroline says again.

"And at home, is everything okay?"

"Yeah." Caroline isn't cooperative, so Robert changes tack. He charitably infers that Carol has got some personal problem. He also infers that, if Carol doesn't want to talk about it, it may be because it's very personal or she's afraid. He decides to apply NVC (Nonviolent Communication).

"Carol, the fact that you are late to the *Dailies* and that you are late in delivering the user story that you've assigned yourself is impacting the performance of the team, so I would like you to tell me what's wrong with you, just to be able to help you. I just want to help you, Carol." Robert emphasizes that he only wants to help Caroline, in case his inference that she was afraid was correct.

At that moment Caroline breaks down crying.

"I'm so sorry, Rob," Caroline answers between sobs. "My mother has become ill. I'm an only child, and she's only got me to take care of her." Robert realizes that he has done well inferring charitably. He tries to get Caroline to go over how it impacts her emotionally, and what she needs so she can pin down a need and Robert is able to help her.

"Wow, I'm so sorry, Carol. And what care does your mother need?"

"Well, I have to take her to the hospital several times a week so they can give her chemo. That's why I've been running late. Then she gets nauseous, and she feels so bad that I've got to be with her until she feels better. She's very weak," Carol says between sobs.

"And how do you feel combining work with the drama you've got at home?"

"Very bad, because I don't focus. I know that I'm delaying the team, and all the trips to the hospital are exhausting me."

"What do you need? How can I help you?"

"On the days my mother has chemo, I'd rather not come to the office, because I'm late and I get very stressed."

Robert thinks that it is time to go straight to an action plan that helps Caroline, since her needs have already been expressed.

"And have you thought what you could do, to balance this situation and not end up getting sick?"

"Teleworking in those days would be great. And on the days that I don't have to go to the hospital, I'd like to arrive very early, so that I can leave very soon and be with my mother longer in the evening."

"Well, talk no more, Carol. Today I will get you a token to be able to telework. If I can't, I'll give you mine, so that, if something breaks, they blame me. But don't worry, everyone knows that Scrum Masters have no idea, so it will seem normal that the connection with my token has broken something." After this silly joke, Robert winks at Caroline, and she starts to smile.

Antonio Montes Orozco

"Thanks a lot, Rob."

"When does your mother have the next chemo session?"

"Tomorrow."

"Well, don't show up at the office tomorrow. Leave the office soon today and go with her. Your mother is the important thing, and this is just work. I also offer to call you when you telework, so you can tell me how your mother is doing and, incidentally, to tell you what news has been in the *Daily*. Do you agree?" This way Robert keeps the team in sync, now that Caroline is going to telework.

"Yeah, thanks a lot, Rob."

"You're welcome, Carol. I'm here to facilitate your work, and make sure that all of you are as good as possible." Robert is overjoyed at having been helpful.

In this Coaching session we have seen again a mixture of techniques. There are times when the interlocutor does not want to collaborate. In these cases, instead of inferring negatively, such as thinking that they're rude, or that they aren't behaving professionally, I encourage you to be **charitable** and always put yourself on the most benign assumption. In this case, Robert has been charitable, and then he has discovered that Caroline had a serious problem, and she was having a very hard time. Posing the question with the NVC steps, making it clear that he only wanted to help, is what has made Caroline react: Robert has shown the objective data, then he's shown the consequences that these had, and has ended up asking directly, remarking that he just wanted to help. Then he's used the NVC technique to make Caroline aware of her real needs, to be able to express them. And, using Powerful Questions, Robert has guided Caroline through GROW, to see what options she had considered. Fortunately, you can telework in the IT world, so Caroline will be able to take care of her mother, and she'll be able to continue helping the team. If Robert had inferred without charity, he would have put Caroline on the defensive and reinforced her belief in being afraid, so she would not have come up with anything clear. In addition, Caroline herself is the one that has solved the problem of combining her work with her family situation, so her commitment is absolute, and Robert is sure that she will get the most out of teleworking.

How to "Be" a Coach

To "be" a real coach it isn't enough to get a certificate, or read this book, or "do Coaching". Coaching skills require training and are difficult to obtain, since the coach has to fight against their cultural baggage and against their Ego.

The amount of skills to learn can be so overwhelming, that it is easy to get discouraged, as the coach will find themselves constantly fighting against the current and against the beliefs burned into our society.

In addition, you'll find that in your environment, apart from you, others do not know how to listen, which can lead to frustration. You will also understand why you have never been able to communicate with that person whom you have labeled, and whom you do not listen to in an egoless way. And you will also understand why it is difficult for you to communicate with those other people who have labeled you, and who filter whatever you say.

But, with patience and perseverance, in the end you will master the art of listening, the art of asking Powerful Questions, and the art of generating action plans and bringing them to fruition. At some point you will be able to help, and that satisfaction will compensate for the frustration of being one of the few around you who knows how to listen and communicate.

Antonio Montes Orozco

Another issue you will come across is the temptation to teach your interlocutors how to listen. That is equivalent to lecturing, and I've already told you that lecturing cuts off communication. Once again, we find that Coaching and Humility go hand in hand. In the end, the coach becomes someone very humble who knows how to help others, and who suffers, with great patience, the aggressions of those who do not know how to listen, or how to talk, or how to make simple requests without using verbal violence.

I'm speaking very negatively about being a coach. I was amused to read in the book *Agile Coaching* by Rachel Davies and Liz Sedley that they advise that we should find a shoulder to cry on, as resistance to change in teams can be frustrating. But the fact that it's hard at the beginning and requires a lot of vocation to help others is not a reason to abandon Coaching. Think about how fulfilling your life will be, and how useful you will feel. In addition, knowing how to talk and listen is a very useful skill in your personal and professional life.

A coach is very close to the **ascetics** that Christianity has given, whose main virtues are **Strength**, to fight against the current; **Temperance**, to patiently endure injustice and resistance to change; and **Humility**, to recognize their own mistakes, their own limitations, and be able to follow a path of Continuous Improvement or even to ask for help.

In order for you to "be" a coach, I propose the following six steps, to make the training smoother. I hope that each step gives you hope and energy to undertake the next one.

Antonio Montes Orozco

FIRST STEP: ASSIMILATING THE THEORY AND OBSERVING

In this book I give you many theoretical touches that must be assimilated. From now on, always keep in mind the principle that **without involvement there is no commitment**. Notice how around you, whether in family, with friends, or at work, if there is no participation, people do not commit.

Internalize the **Ladder of Inference**. Notice how quickly people label with few data and facts. Also notice how people confuse judgments and opinions with objective data and facts. Remember, just watching, never lecture. Internalize the **NVC** (Nonviolent Communication) procedure. Notice how people make requests by orally attacking, labeling, and being defensive. On these occasions it is a good time to review the steps of the NVC: understanding the data that our interlocutor has observed, empathizing with the emotions that they report, understanding their needs, and facilitating their request. Remember, just observe; at the most ask to collect data, since we are in the assimilation and observation phase. Take out all your Humility and bury your pride to ward off the temptation to give a master class on how to make requests without violence.

Internalize the procedure of giving **feedback**. Remember that it is a gift, so you only have to give it with the consent of your interlocutor, and you must be open to the possibility of being denied it. The usual around us, both in family and professional environments, will be that they give us feedback without asking for permission, and that they also confuse "being" with "doing." Once more, just observe, learn from others' mistakes, and take notes to be ready when it's your turn to give feedback.

When the team always manifests the same points in *Retrospectives*, remember the **OSAR** model of the observer and consider whether it is time to change the observer (Second Order Learning), or if it's time to change beliefs (Transformational Learning), or even if it's time to change the system (what I call Learning of Base).

Learn to identify the nine **Cognitive Distortions** that I've taught you, observe how people around us sometimes use irrational reasoning. Identify when victim language is being used and when responsible language is. Again, just listen and watch without accusing your interlocutor of using irrational reasoning or victim language, and without lecturing. Remember: Strength, Temperance, and much, much Humility.

Lastly, flee from **psychoanalysis**. You are simply observing and learning. You have to do it so subtly that your interlocutor should never have the feeling that you are psychoanalyzing them. If your interlocutor notices, they will feel attacked and will end up being irritated, and with good reason. Increasing your doses of Humility will lead you to observe in silence, without having to demonstrate everything you have learned in this book, and therefore without irritating your interlocutor.

As a proposal, I put forward that you analyze the conversations of different films and TV shows, as they are full of misunderstandings, verbal attacks and poorly made inferences based on wrong data. Think about what you would say if you were in the same situation as the scenes.

This first step of observation can take several weeks or even months. When you are fully aware of the theory that I've explained, it's time to jump into learning new skills, and the most important thing for a coach is knowing how to listen properly.

SECOND STEP: LEARNING TO LISTEN WITH EMPATHY AND WITHOUT EGO

For a while we've been observing how we communicate and how others communicate. We've got a good theoretical base, and we already know all the way we have to go. It's time to start listening training.

We've seen the listening levels, and I've explained that it is best to forget about ourselves (**egoless** listening), focusing exclusively on understanding everything that we are told, and on empathizing with our interlocutor, forcing ourselves not to apply our filters or beliefs. We will intervene only to ask and paraphrase when we want to clarify doubts, or when we want to confirm that we are understanding well.

As this skill costs a lot to train, the fastest way to learn is by egoless listening to everyone, both family members, friends, co-workers, and strangers.

The first step is eye contact: force yourself to look everyone you talk to **directly in the eye**.

Our enemy is our **pride**. It is like an imp perched on our shoulder, constantly reminding us how good we are and how extensive our knowledge is, encouraging us to intervene and demonstrate everything we know. That's why I've told you throughout the chapters how important **Humility** is. In order to have inner peace, we do not need to show what we are worth and that justice is done: simply by being humble and giving prominence to our interlocutor we will discover the peace that small act of love gives us. Also, if we manage to help, we will be the happiest and fullest people in the world.

Another enemy is **lack of time**. If we are in a hurry, we will despair of seeing our interlocutor roll up and not stop talking. At that moment the imp that we have perched on our shoulder will attack and invite us to label them as annoying. Labeling is no longer egoless listening, so I invite you to make yourself predictable and to advise that you have very little time, or to postpone the conversation for another more propitious moment.

Little by little, the Powerful Questions that will lead you to understand everything and to empathize with your interlocutor will come out without thinking.

Antonio Montes Orozco

This step will cost you more, as we have an almost unhealthy tendency to filter and infer, even before our interlocutor opens their mouth. So arm yourself with Strength and Temperance; you are going to need them.

THIRD STEP: TRAINING IN THE NVC

Now that we are clear about our shortcomings, and we have learned to listen properly, it is time to train in the NVC (Nonviolent Communication).

Training in making requests using the NVC is very easy, and in a few days, you can have this technique internalized so that it comes out automatically.

If you regularly have trouble communicating with someone when making requests, you will be impressed with how effective this technique is. NVC is especially effective in the family environment.

Exposing the objective data, showing how they make us feel, expressing our needs, and launching the request politely is something that our interlocutor will always welcome, so you will quickly see value in it.

In the same way, you can train yourself in guiding your interlocutor to review these four steps so that they fulfill their need, so that you can make an offer to help them. Remember that this is not about lecturing on how to ask for things but using Powerful Questions to guide: "What happened?" "How did it make you feel?" "What do you need?" "How can I help you?"

As I've mentioned before, this ability will be internalized very soon and will encourage you to continue.

FOURTH STEP: LEARNING TO GO UP AND DOWN THE LADDER OF INFERENCE

At this moment you know how to listen in an egoless way; you've been observing around you the way people communicate; and you have discovered, in yourself and in others, all the errors that lead us to not knowing how to communicate. In addition, you dominate the NVC, and you're capable of making requests and detecting needs to make offers. It is time to guide your training towards going up and down the Ladder of Inference.

We will go down the ladder to discover the beliefs that led to the actions we observe. Remember not to read minds, as it is impossible, and it is also an irrational practice. Instead ask Powerful Questions: "I've detected that you've got this belief. Is that so?"

Detecting beliefs gives us an advantage in conversations because, if we see that a belief is false and blocks our interlocutor, we can reassure them, making them see that the reality is different, thus opening a door to hope.

We'll go up the ladder to act, but stay focused on objective data and facts. By the way, you will begin to train yourself to realize how far from reality our judgments and opinions can be. Therefore, I recommend that you check your inferences whenever you can.

"I assume you're angry. Is that so?" we ask.

"No, I'm happy. What happens is that I get that ugly when I smile," they answer us, to our amazement.

That's why I recommend you to be **charitable**, always seeking the most benign inference.

Since I was a boy, I've been taught how good it is to have "psychology", to be able to read thought accurately. Now I realize the absurdity of this belief. In the first place it is irrational to pretend to have that mind-reading ability, and you are really hiding fear of life and an insane desire for protection. And secondly, it is unwise to infer without objective data, and it will lead us to make mistakes most of the time.

It amazes me that popular wisdom encourages these fallacious practices through sayings like "think wrong and you will be right." In addition to becoming an ascetic, you will have to abandon lots of popular beliefs that take us away from the philosophy of Coaching.

FIFTH STEP: LEARNING TO BE TRUSTWORTHY

Since you started your training, you've learned how many mistakes you used to make when it came to communicating and listening. That is an important blow for our Ego, which is good, because it gives us Humility, which is so necessary for the coach.

Also, by controlling yourself so much to egoless listening and keeping quiet, you are generating a lot of Temperance. You already had the Strength trained, and that is why you decided to learn the arts of Coaching.

The only thing left is for others to see you as highly trustworthy. I have devoted an entire chapter to trust, as it is the key to your relationship with the team. Be honest, don't hesitate to show your vulnerabilities, and make yourself predictable.

Trust is a very difficult treasure to obtain, and very easy to lose. There are no secrets or tricks here, so it must be born out of honest sincerity and transparency.

All the Humility that you have generated these weeks will help you show your vulnerabilities. You are trained to bury your pride, and you do not mind making mistakes in public, humbly acknowledging them, and instantly asking for forgiveness. You are an ascetic: an example for your team, a great leader.

SIXTH STEP: HAVING TRAINING COACHING SESSIONS

The best way to learn is doing, to make mistakes and learn from them. There is no other method. Now you have realized the problems that communication poses, you know how to listen, you master NVC, you control the ladder of inference and you are trustworthy: it is time to launch into Coaching sessions.

A very good way to practice is to find a colleague who is also a Scrum Master and who also wants to train in the art of Coaching. And additionally, if you have both read this book, all the better.

You can meet for coffee. One plays the role of coach and the other one the role of coachee. After the session, you can give feedback between the two of you. On successive days you can repeat the session, swapping roles.

This practice will give you the ability to know which Powerful Questions apply at each time, so that you will use them automatically.

SUMMARY

I have proposed six steps for you to become a coach.

- **First step: Assimilating the theory and observing**. Learn the theory by heart and watch how the people around communicate, including yourself. Extend this observation to the movies and series you watch. Remember, you are just observing, not lecturing nor demonstrating what you have learned in this book.

- **Second step**: **Learning to listen actively with empathy and without Ego**. This is the main quality of the coach: knowing how to listen, empathizing with the interlocutor, forgetting themselves and their filters, and avoiding judging.

- **Third step**: **Training in the NVC**. NVC is easy to master and it will encourage you to apply it, and see how well it works. In addition, you can help others, making offers based on their needs.

- **Fourth step**: **Learning to go up and down the ladder of inference**. This way you will be able to detect the data and beliefs that led to the actions that you've observed, and you'll also be aware of the inferences that are made based on the observed data.

- **Fifth Step**: **Learning to be trustworthy**. There is no secret: reliability is based on sincerity and transparency.

- **Sixth Step**: **Having Coaching Training sessions**. I recommend that you have the sessions with a fellow Scrum Master who has also read this book. You can have multiple sessions to switch roles.

Conclusion

We've concluded this exciting journey through the world of Coaching applied to Agilism. We've learned that, around us, there is no knowledge of how to listen and converse effectively. It is the great cross that coaches will have to carry, but it is precisely a cross that provides the satisfaction of being the only one who can help, simply because being the only one who knows how to listen and motivate.

Each theoretical chapter I have tried to complement with examples so that the concepts remain clear.

In order not to force you to go back in the book, I have reminded you of the key concepts, so that you could always move forward.

Aware of how little time we have today, I have tried to condense all the theory and examples into a short, quickly read book.

After seeing the theory, I've shown you two practical examples on how to apply what you've learned. I hope these examples have clarified the concepts for you.

I've also suggested six steps to "be" a coach, so that you gradually transform yourself into an ascetic Agilist.

I wish you a full and happy life, and I hope this book contributes to that. To you, my infinite thanks.

Antonio Montes Orozco

Special Thanks

First of all I'm going to thank Fernando Vargas Sánchez, my great teacher, for all the teachings he's given me about Coaching. Without him this book would never have seen the light. Fer, I will always be eternally grateful for your generosity, and for your great talent in transmitting your extensive knowledge to me.

Second, I'm going to thank Juan Manuel Gómez Ramos for all his teachings. JuanMa, you have been an example for me, and from you I have learned your values and your great professional ethics. You are my reference as an Agile Coach.

Third, I'm going to thank Marta San Martín Arribas for everything she has taught me with her great example. Marta, you have always been the best coach in your environment, and my great teacher. I fondly remember your Coaching courses and the professionalism with which you faced new challenges.

And last but not least, I thank you, dear reader, for reading this book. I hope it helps you both in your personal life and in your professional one.

To all, my heartfelt thanks.

Antonio Montes Orozco

About the Author

Antonio Montes Orozco was born in Madrid, Spain, in 1972. He studied Telecommunications Engineering at the Polytechnic University of Madrid.

He began his first steps in the world of work as a systems administrator, specializing in the Solaris, HPUX and AIX operating systems. After a few years as a systems administrator, he started programming in C++ and, in 2006, he learned about the Scrum methodology. He was one of the pioneers in its application in Spain. Since then he has been working as a Scrum Master and as a coach to implement this methodology.

He ended up working in a major Spanish financial institution, where he introduced Scrum in one of the Business areas.

He was certified in 2015 by the prestigious PMI (Project Management Institute), as a practitioner of Agile (ACP: Agile Certified Practitioner), and by Scrum Manager in 2014.

In 2016 he obtained the Executive Master in Management of Information Technologies by the Institute of Business Executives (IDE-CESEM) of Spain.

In 2020 he obtained the Master Coaching & Mentoring Fundamentals for Agile by the European School of Coaching (EEC) of Spain, being certified as a coach by the prestigious ICF (International Couching Foundation).

Antonio Montes Orozco

Credits

Agile Coaching for Scrum Masters: Learn the main concepts of Coaching that Scrum Masters need to know.

Antonio Montes Orozco

It is not allowed the total or partial reproduction of this book, nor its incorporation to a computer system, nor its transmission in any form or by any means, be it electronic, mechanical, by photocopy, by recording or other methods, without prior permission, and in writing from the editor. The infringement of the aforementioned rights may constitute an offense against intellectual property.

© cover design, SelfPubBookCovers.com/BravoCovers, 2020

© Antonio Montes Orozco, 2020

First edition in e-book: November 2020

ISBN: 9798569675746